PLANET EARTH

AMERICAN
MOUNTAINS
AND CANYONS

WILLIAM K SMITHEY

GALLERY BOOKS
An Imprint of W. H. Smith Publishers Inc.
112 Madison Avenue
New York City 10016

Text
William K. Smithey

Editorial
Pauline Graham

Design
Clive Dorman

Production
Ruth Arthur
David Proffit
Sally Connolly
Andrew Whitelaw

Jacket Design
Claire Leighton

Commissioning Editor
Andrew Preston

Director of Production
Gerald Hughes

Publishing Assistant
Edward Doling

Director of Publishing
David Gibbon

Photography
Planet Earth Pictures:
Franz J. Camenzind front cover, 6, 10, 15 *bottom*, 17, 28 *bottom*, 30;
Mary Clay 12 *top*, 13 *top*, 16 *top*, 22, 31 *bottom*, back cover;
Richard Coomber 14; John Downer 15 *top*, 27;
John Fawcett 29 *bottom*; D. Robert Franz 31 *top*; Dr. Peter Gasson
25 *bottom*, 28 *top*; Robert Jureit 7 *top left*, 25 *top*, 26, 32;
Ned Kelly 7 *bottom*; A. Kerstitch 19; Dave Lyons 23 *top,* 24;
David A. Ponton 12 *bottom*, 13 *bottom*, 18 *bottom*;
David E. Rowley 7, 11 *top right*, 16 *bottom*, 18 *top*, 20, 21 *bottom*,
23 *top*, 29 *top*; William K. Smithey 8, 9; Peter Stevenson 5;
Dorian Weisel 4; Joyce Wilson 10-11 *top*, 21 *top*.

CLB 2488
This edition published in 1990 by Gallery Books,
an imprint of WH Smith Publishers, Inc,
112 Madison Avenue, New York 10016.
Colour separations by Scantrans Pte Ltd, Singapore.
Printed and bound by New Interlitho, Italy.
ISBN 0 8317 6980 7

Gallery Books are available for bulk purchase for sales promotions
and premium use. For details write or telephone
the Manager of Special Sales, WH Smith Publishers, Inc,
112 Madison Avenue, New York, New York 10016 (212) 532-6600.

CONTENTS

INTRODUCTION

From a human viewpoint the earth seems complete, frozen in time. Only occasionally, such as when a volcano shudders to life or an earthquake rattles our cities, are we reminded how restless the earth truly is. But these events, dramatic as they can be, are just hints of the forces that have sculpted the earth, constantly changing it throughout the billions of years of geologic time.

The neat, almost jigsaw-puzzle "fit" of the coastlines of western Africa and eastern South America is more than a coincidence. The earth's continents were once joined in a supercontinent that broke apart about 230 million years ago. The theory of plate tectonics – the idea that the earth's crust is composed of separate, moving plates that grind against or pull apart from one another – explains continental drift.

The idea of collisions between plates also explains much about the formation of mountains. As the heavier crust of the ocean floor pushes under the lighter continental crust, volcanoes form. Heat from the enormous friction caused by these collisions creates the magma which fuels volcanic eruptions. The young mountain ranges of western North America formed as the continent drifted west and collided with other plates.

Water is usually responsible for the erosion that forms valleys, canyons and gorges. Glaciers, now confined to the north, once extended to more southerly locations where they sculpted much of the alpine scenery. The Colorado River has relentlessly eroded a swath through the plateaus of Arizona, revealing strata of rock formed over one billion years ago. The ancient Appalachian Mountains of eastern North America, now reduced to long low ridges and valleys by millions of years of exposure to the elements, may once have stood as tall as today's Himalayas.

Below: magma erupts from a fissure on the island of Hawaii. Facing page: Yosemite Falls plunge 2,565 feet into glacier-carved Yosemite Valley.

MAJOR NORTH AMERICAN MOUNTAIN RANGES

MOUNTAINS OF ALASKA

The mountains of Alaska give the state much of its wilderness character. The Brooks Range, the most northerly, runs east-west for nearly the full width of Alaska, protecting the central part of the state from the severity of the Arctic. To the south lies the Alaska Range, which includes Denali, also known as Mount McKinley – North America's highest peak.

The coast of Alaska is also defined by its mountains. The eighty Aleutian Islands, which curve westward from the mainland dividing the Pacific Ocean from the Bering Sea, are part of a mountain range formed by recent volcanism. The Chugach and Saint Elias mountains, along with the Fairweather Range, form the rugged, southern coast.

THE OLYMPICS

Great forests of conifers ring the snow-capped peaks of the Olympic Range to the west of Seattle, Washington. The Olympics are a compact range, created by a collision between two pieces of the earth's crust and covering an area just fifty by thirty-five miles. Six glaciers descend from the slopes of Mount Olympus which, at nearly 8,000 feet, is the tallest peak in the range.

THE CASCADES

From Mount Lassen in northern California to southwestern Canada stretches a string of colossal volcanoes known as the Cascade Range. Two Cascade volcanoes, Mount Saint Helens and Lassen Peak, have erupted in recent years. Three others, Mount Baker, Mount Washington and Mount Rainier, erupted minor amounts of steam and rock fragments in the mid-1800s and still occasionally emit quantities of steam and gas.

In 1980, Mount Saint Helens was dramatically altered by the same forces that had created it. The eruption, which formed a new volcanic vent at its summit, was powerful and unexpectedly focused, blowing up a hurricane wind of scalding gases and superheated rock to the west and north. Along this quadrant, trees were uprooted or broken as far distant from the mountain as seventeen miles.

Below: 20,320-foot-tall Denali peak. Facing page top: (left) the Olympic Range, and (right) Lassen Peak in the Cascades. Facing page bottom: the destruction wreaked by the eruption of Mount Saint Helens.

THE SIERRA NEVADA

The Sierra Nevada extends for about 400 miles within the state of California, covering an area greater than that of the French, Swiss and Italian alps combined. It is a dominant feature of California, separating the Central Valley to the west from the arid Great Basin to the east.

Throughout much of their length the Sierras exist as a single main divide with separate watersheds draining to the east and west sides. At its southern culmination, however, it is a complex of high peaks – some paralleling the main divide, others branching from it. Many of these secondary crests, which include the Ritter Range, Cathedral Range and the Great Western Divide, by themselves would be considered major mountain ranges.

The Sierra Nevada was formed when an enormous block of the earth's crust rose on the east side, causing a tilt to the west. As a result the range is asymmetrical with a broad, gently ascending western flank and a steep eastern side. Summit elevations increase steadily from north to south, culminating at 14,495-foot-high Mount Whitney, the tallest American peak outside Alaska.

BASIN AND RANGE

The basin and range area between the Cascade and Sierra Nevada mountain ranges to the west and the Rockies to the east, contains approximately 160 different mountain ranges. In some areas, peaks project from the high desert valleys to heights of more than a mile, with mountains ranging in elevation from 9,000 feet to over 14,000 feet.

Facing page: Half Dome, Yosemite Valley. Mount Whitney (below) dominates the Alabama Hills in Owens Valley.

THE ROCKY MOUNTAINS

The Rocky Mountains, or Great Divide, separates bodies of waters destined for the Atlantic from those headed for the Pacific. This is the longest and most easterly of the great western mountain ranges. The Rockies begin in the north with the Brooks Range of northern Alaska and extend south to central New Mexico, and they continue, with some interruption, all the way to the South American Andes.

The Rocky Mountains in fact consist of several lesser ranges, each with its own identity. To the north is the Bitterroot Range of Idaho and Montana and the Big Horn Mountains of Montana and Wyoming. The Central Rocky Mountains of Wyoming are punctuated by the Grand Tetons, which climb sharply from the surrounding flatlands. The southern Rockies of western Colorado comprise a broad complex of mountains with more than fifty peaks over 14,000 feet tall. Four major rivers, the Platte, Arkansas, Rio Grande and Colorado, originate among these mountains.

THE APPALACHIANS

Compared to the mountains of the West, the peaks of the Appalachians are less than half as high. The Appalachians stretch for over 2,000 miles – from Newfoundland south through the Berkshires of Massachusetts and New York's Catskills, continuing through the Blue Ridge Mountains of Virginia, the Cumberlands and the Great Smoky Mountains of Tennessee.

Unlike mountains to the north, the southern Appalachians have escaped the glaciers of repeated ice ages. As a result, the luxuriant, mixed hardwood forests of this area are the magnificent result of millions of years of uninterrupted development.

The Great Smoky Mountains (left) of Tennessee derive their name from the atmospheric haze created by the trees. Below: the Grand Tetons, one of sixty ranges comprising the Rocky Mountain chain. Below left: Logan Pass, in the Rocky Mountains of Glacier National Park, Montana, sculpted by recent glaciers.

THE MOUNTAIN ENVIRONMENT

Mountains create their own weather; their height interferes with and alters wind and storm systems as they pass. As a storm front meets a mountain range it is forced upward, resulting in significantly more precipitation over the mountains than over the surrounding lowlands. Because the temperature falls with increasing altitude, mountains are naturally colder than lowlands. Similarly, the climate becomes cooler as one travels north. To climb a mountain from desert floor to summit is comparable, in terms of climate, to journeying from central Mexico to the Arctic.

The relationship of altitude, latitude and climate is seen in various ways. Timberline – the level above which it is too cold in the summer for trees to grow – occurs, in the central Sierra Nevada, above 10,000 feet, while further north, on Washington State's Mount Rainier, trees cannot live at altitudes above 7,000 feet. Some characteristically northern plant and animal species will flourish in the cooler environments that prevail over the tops of mountain peaks found in the otherwise warm south.

Steller's jay (above) is common in western mountains. Below: lightning charges the sky during a summer storm in the Rocky Mountains.

ANIMALS AND ELEVATION

While some animal species can range from low valleys all the way up to the timberline, most are more limited in the range of altitudes that they can tolerate. Directly, or indirectly, this is attributable to climate.

Because their body temperature reflects that of the environment, most reptiles and amphibians cannot survive the severe cold that prevails through much of the year near the timberline. The distribution of plants is directly affected by climate and indirectly, therefore, the animals that depend on them. The snowshoe rabbit resides in high, coniferous forests and is ill adapted for life in lower, scrubbier conditions.

Three species of jays: scrub, pinyon and Steller's, as well as the closely related Clark's nutcracker, occur in the Sierra Nevada. These birds are similar in habit but avoid direct competition with each other by occupying areas of different altitude. Likewise the dusky-footed woodrat lives in the Sierra foothills and low-elevation mountains, while the bushy-tailed woodrat predominates in the upper forest.

The scrub jay (above) is found at the lower elevations of western mountain ranges. Low growth characterizes alpine plants (below left).

THE ALPINE REALM

Extending from the timberline to the tops of the highest peaks, the alpine-realm environment is a cold and desolate place. This is the harshest mountain environment, characterized by expanses of bare rock dotted with low, sparse vegetation. Alpine climates feature long, snowy winters followed by short growing seasons.

Because there is neither time nor light and warmth enough to fuel the energy needed for large plants to grow, most alpine plants grow to only an inch or two in height. Many, such as pussypaws, have a low, circular growth form, which allows them to obtain sunlight from all directions and to take advantage of the increased degree of warmth at ground level.

Due to a lack of food and shelter, few animals reside in the alpine zone. The rosy finch is an exception. Though it may leave the alpine area during the severest part of winter, the rest of the year it is as likely to be found above the tree line as below it. In the Sierra Nevada the rosy finch is a true high-altitude resident, rarely occurring below 9,500 feet. It builds a nest among rock crevices and eats seeds and insects blown uphill by the almost constant alpine wind.

WESTERN MOUNTAIN MEADOW

Meadows are clearings in the forest. Some began as glacier-carved lakes, eventually filled in by silt and vegetation. Other areas are naturally treeless; they may be too wet, too cold or too dry to support tree seedlings. Meadows may also form in the aftermath of a fire or an avalanche.

Wet meadows form when the water table – or the level below which the ground is saturated with water – is near the surface. These meadows are often found adjacent to lakes or streams and, because the soil is usually cold and soggy, only moisture-tolerant plants such as rushes, willows, grasses and sedges can survive.

Often large and grassy, dry meadows are usually found on ridge tops or on south-facing slopes where the soil is well drained. These are usually fed by melting snow and, after the spring runoff, they dry out quickly.

Mountain meadows are grassy islands surrounded by a sea of trees. The mixing of these two different environments, the open space and nutritious vegetation of the meadow with the shelter and seeds of the forest, results in an exceptionally good place to find wildlife

Small mammals are abundant in meadows and, with minimum cover, they have developed various strategies to avoid predators. Some, such as the meadow vole, tunnel under the dense tangle made by the blades of sedges and grasses. Others, including badgers, ground squirrels and gophers, burrow underground to avoid being eaten.

The Belding's ground squirrel is a conspicuous meadow mammal which is especially numerous in the Tuolumne Meadows area of Yosemite National Park. Its nickname of "picket pin" results from its habit of standing upright next to its burrow openings, scanning the area for predators.

The northern pocket gopher has short, muscular legs with crescent-shaped claws – a combination perfectly adapted for digging through sandy, meadow soil. Their burrows consist of a horizontal main tunnel branched with many short passages which they use either to store food or as further exits to the surface. Nest chambers are built at the end of vertical shafts sinking about two feet below the surface. Pocket gophers eat underground tubers and roots as well as succulent green leaves gathered from the meadow's surface.

Cooper's and red-tailed hawks, northern harriers, goshawks, golden eagles, merlins and the American kestrel hunt meadow rodents by day, while at night the great horned owl becomes the dominant airborne predator. Tree or violet-green swallows fly the meadow hunting insects by day. Bats take over from them at night.

White-crowned sparrows and mountain bluebirds restrict their feeding areas almost entirely to meadows. The white-crowned sparrow nests either along the meadow's edge or in willow thickets, while the bluebird uses abandoned woodpecker holes in trees near the meadow. The American robin nests near meadows and hunts for earthworms and other invertebrates.

Hummingbirds feed on flower nectar and, in turn, the pollen which dusts them fertilizes the next flower they visit. Because the relationship is mutually beneficial, flowers have evolved brightly colored red, orange or yellow flowers which are tubular in shape to attract and accommodate hummingbirds. In turn, hummingbirds have evolved a hovering type of flight which allows them to feed from the delicate blossoms.

North America's smallest bird, the tiny calliope hummingbird, weighs only one tenth of an ounce. To satisfy the needs of their high metabolic rates they visit many meadow wildflowers, such as Indian paintbrushes, penstemon, red columbine, monkeyflower and manzanita, feeding from as many as 1,000 blossoms in a day.

Below: a mountain meadow blooming in the Grand Tetons, Wyoming. Facing page: (top) a golden eagle soars over open terrain, searching for prey, and (bottom) badgers. These delightful predators feed on ground squirrels and pocket gophers.

WILDLIFE OF MOUNTAIN CLIFFS

The boulders that fall and accumulate at the base of cliffs provide a habitat for a variety of small animals. In the higher elevations of western North America, pikas are common on slopes of talus, or rock debris, formed by smaller rocks. Pikas leave the talus to forage for green plants, eating some on the spot and carrying the rest back to the boulders near their den where they spread the plants to dry for later use.

Marmots are the largest members of the squirrel family, but unlike squirrels feed entirely on grasses or other green plants. Two species, the yellow-bellied marmot and the more northerly hoary marmot, are common on rocky or talus slopes in western mountains, while the woodchuck, also known as the groundhog, is found in the meadows and woods of the Southern Appalachians and throughout the eastern states.

Except for the woodchuck, which is a solitary animal, marmots are social creatures. They emerge in mid-May, fitting the entire year's activity into the warm, summer months. When startled, they retreat to their dens, often standing near the entrance sounding a characteristic whistle. By early October they have usually stored enough fat to spend the harsh winter hibernating, conserving energy by lowering their body temperature and

slowing their heart rate.

Other animals live on the cliff face. Violet-green swallows make their nest of weed stems, grasses and feathers on the face of sheer cliffs. They feed entirely on insects, including flies, ants, wasps, bees and moths.

Mountain goats spend much of their time on or

near cliffs. These shaggy goats, which are closely related to the European chamois, are descendants of stock that arrived from Asia via the Bering land bridge and are now found throughout the northwestern mountains from Alaska to Idaho. They expertly navigate steep terrain using their specially adapted hoofs.

While mountain goats are native to the Cascade Range, they were absent from the isolated Olympic Peninsula until the 1920s, when a dozen animals were transported there from Canada. They have flourished, multiplying to the point where they are threatening the area's natural vegetation.

Bighorn sheep are also common on craggy mountain peaks. In their mating ritual combats the males use their massive horns, set in extra thick skulls, to stage spectacular head-butting contests. The horn size determines the status of the male and contests most often occur between rams with similar sized horns.

As with their close relatives the desert bighorn sheep, mountain bighorn numbers have suffered from the presence of man and his introduction to their habitats of domestic sheep. Man's activities caused sheep to take refuge in ever smaller areas, increasing competition between bighorn and other grazers. Moreover, domestic sheep, brought to mountain meadows for summer pasture, infected the native sheep with diseases imported from Europe.

Facing page: (top) a mountain goat, master of his precarious realm, and (bottom) a pair of Rocky Mountain bighorn sheep. Note their massive horns and the greater size of the male. Related to rabbits and hares, the pica (above) lives on high talus slopes. Below: a mother yellow-bellied marmot and her young.

Hawk Mountain, Pennsylvania

After leaving their breeding grounds in the northern United States and Canada, many different birds of prey soar south through the eastern Appalachians along Kittatinny Ridge and past the Hawk Mountain Sanctuary. On a clear fall day, with the wind from the northwest, thousands of hawks can be observed passing this spur along the ridge.

The most plentiful of the Hawk Mountain migrants is the broad-winged hawk: as many as 20,000 pass in a day on their way south to winter in the tropics of South America. They are small, crow-sized birds that hunt mainly in woods, taking snakes, mice, frogs, toads and other small prey. Northern goshawks, as well as Cooper's and sharp-shinned hawks, are also commonly seen.

After breeding in the dense deciduous and boreal forests of eastern America, the broad-winged hawk (right) winters in South America. Cooper's hawk (below), an inhabitant of broken woodlands and streamside groves of deciduous trees, migrates along ridges and coastlines.

Mountain Islands

The earth's changing climate has left some species stranded on top of mountains. During the last ice age, as recently as 10,000 years ago, the Great Basin was a cooler and wetter place than it is today. As the climate became drier, the mountain peaks that interrupt the nearly endless sagebrush of the Great Basin remained relatively moist – in effect, creating island habitats separated from each other by the arid desert surrounding them.

While large species, such as deer, coyote and mountain lions, can cross the large desert areas that separate the mountain ranges; smaller animals, such as the purplish copper and checkerspot butterflies, cannot. Isolated as they are, with no new species to replenish them, the small animals of these Great Basin islands may eventually disappear, wiped out by a particularly bad winter or a prolonged drought.

Below: a buckeye butterfly, and (right) a painted lady butterfly.

Mountain Birds

Bald Eagle

The tale of the bald eagle has become a rare success story. Once seriously diminished in numbers throughout the lower forty-eight states due to shooting, pesticides and human encroachment, intensive efforts of conservationists have recently led to a substantial recovery.

Bald eagles are most often seen on the coast or near rivers and lakes where they feed mainly on fish which they either catch for themselves or steal from ospreys. They construct large nests, up to seven or eight feet across and twelve feet deep. Although they prefer trees, they sometimes nest on rocky promontories. On islands they will even nest on the ground.

Three thousand or more bald eagles gather each year during October, November and December along several miles of the Chilkat River of southeastern Alaska. This spectacular assemblage is the largest known gathering of bald eagles, attracted by the spent carcasses of the late-fall run of salmon.

California Condor

The California condor is a huge bird, with a wingspan larger than any other North American land bird to enable it to ride warm air currents. It is so big that, seen head-on, it was often mistaken for an aircraft. However, it is a living fossil, a relic that reached its population peak a million years or more ago when it ranged over the west from Canada to Baja California and across the south to Florida. The last of the wild California condors survived in the rugged canyons, gorges and forested mountains of Southern California.

Today this condor no longer exists in the wild, having fallen victim to habitat loss, shooting and secondary poisoning from affected coyote carcasses. Condors are scavengers and, after their wild food source diminished as California was settled, they survived on dead cattle. The decline of cattle ranches in Southern California finally contributed to their demise.

When their numbers declined to dangerously low levels, the remaining few birds were captured, amid much controversy, and transferred to a captive breeding program. As their numbers slowly increase, their habitat nonetheless continues to be reduced by California's rapid urbanization, making the prospects seem dim for a successful future reintroduction of the California condor to the wild.

Grouse

Most birds avoid the inevitable winter food shortages by leaving the high country for areas more low-lying, or by migrating – leaving the area entirely. One among this yearly exodus, the blue grouse is a distinct anomaly.

After spending its summers in the mixed coniferous forests of the Sierra Nevada and Rocky Mountains, feeding on berries, grasshoppers, beetles and caterpillars, the blue grouse, unusually, moves upslope during the late summer and fall to spend the winter in the upper reaches of the forest. Here it roosts in the dense foliage of the red fir and feeds exclusively on red-fir needles through the winter months.

The ruffed grouse is found from the northern tree limit across North America and south along the major mountain chains. In the summer the ruffed grouse spends its time on the ground, feeding on berries and fruits. With the snows of winter it takes to the treetops and forages on buds and twigs, particularly aspen and poplar.

Right: the distinctive head of a bald eagle. Facing page: (top) a bald eagle roosts on the branch of a dead tree, and (bottom) a ruffed grouse winters high in the mountains.

MOUNTAIN MAMMALS

WILD HOGS

Thousands of European wild boars roam the Appalachian Mountains, thriving in eastern Tennessee and western North Carolina. They are destructive foreigners, wrecking the landscape wherever they are found, and are prized by hunters.

Wild boars, which can weigh more than 200 pounds, are opportunists, eating almost anything. Their diet includes berries, tubers and acorns, as well as carrion and invertebrates. They will also eat snakes, small, native animals and even white-tailed dear fawns. While foraging for food the hogs are extremely disruptive, they compete with the native wildlife, such as deer and turkeys, and are known to destroy the eggs of wild turkeys and grouse.

The spots on a mountain lion kitten (below) are lost in its first six months. This is the most widely ranging species in the New World, found from Canada to the tip of South America.

MOUNTAIN LION

Also known as cougar, puma and panther, the mountain lion is the second-largest cat in the Western Hemisphere – its size is exceeded only by the jaguar of South and Central America. It is a solitary, strongly territorial hunter that requires isolated, prey-rich wilderness in order to survive. Historically, the mountain lion ranged throughout American forests, preferring to feed on young deer and elk, but also eating coyotes, beaver, mice, marmots and hares. Cattle and sheep ranchers who lost small numbers of their animals to the mountain lion, succeeded in having most Western states place bounties on the cat. Widely hunted and poisoned in areas where it came into contact with man, it is now generally limited to remote, mountainous areas.

Facing page: (top) the mixed forest of Gore Canyon in the Colorado Rockies, and (bottom) centuries of geologic history revealed in the strata of the Grand Canyon.

Canyons
Canyons of the Southwest

From its Rocky Mountain origins, the Southwest's major river, the Colorado, cuts its way toward the Gulf of California. As it wears its way through the vast plateaus of northern Arizona it further forms the Grand Canyon of the Colorado River, a spectacle remarkable for its size and unmatched in the complexity of its landforms.

The Grand Canyon is not a simple straight-walled canyon but one with an infinite variety of slopes, cliffs and terraces that reflect the varying degrees of hardness of the underlying rock. The Colorado River runs through a narrow Inner Gorge, varying in depth from 3,500 to 6,000 feet below the canyon rim. Along the canyon's 280-mile length the rim varies from 6,000 to 8,500 feet in height above the floor. The distance across the canyon ranges from four to over fifteen miles, averaging ten.

To travel along the Colorado River as it winds through the Grand Canyon is to take a journey

back through over one billion years of geologic time. At the start of the canyon, near Lee's Ferry, the Colorado has exposed limestone deposited 250 million years ago by ancient oceans. Eighty miles further on, over a mile below the rim, relentless erosion has cut a swath through volcanic rocks which are 1.7 billion years old.

Hiking up to the North Rim from the Colorado River – a climb of 6,000 feet – provides the visitor with a dramatic experience of the varied climates of North America. Along the cooler floor are forests of ponderosa pine, Douglas fir and aspen. Higher up, these give way to more arid forests of pinyon pines and junipers. At the rim, true desert species, such as agave and prickly pear cactus, are found.

The high plateaus of the Grand Canyon are part of the vast Colorado Plateau which covers some 130,000 square miles in the Four Corners region of Colorado, Utah, Arizona and New Mexico. This is Canyon Country, a region of outstanding scenery which includes the National Parks of Bryce and Zion canyons, Monument Valley, Capitol Reef, Arches and another master work by the Colorado River, Canyonlands National Park.

GRAND CANYON WILDLIFE

Together, the Canyon and River pose a significant barrier to the movement of some animals from one side to the other. For example, the Kaibab squirrel and red squirrel are found only to the north of the River, while the spotted ground squirrel and the Gunnison prairie dog are limited to the south.

For obvious reasons, the Canyon is no barrier to the free movement of birds. The Colorado River provides important habitats for migrating waterfowl, among them the common goldeneye, mallard and common merganser. The high-rim forests are home to residents such as the pine siskin and the green-tailed towhee. The American kestrel is the most common hawk along the River.

Today the canyon portion of the Colorado is fed with cold water from Lake Powell. Along with the introduction of game fish, such as rainbow and brown trout, the cold water has driven native fish from the main river into its warmer tributaries. One such fish, the humpback chub – named for its pronounced knob of muscle tissue, is a rare and endangered fish now found only where the Little Colorado River meets the main River.

Facing page: (top) eroded spires, or hoodoos, along Bryce Canyon, and (bottom) Canyonlands National Park. Above: Double Arch, Arches National Monument, and (below) a golden-mantled ground squirrel juvenile standing to attention. It is easily distinguished from a chipmunk by its lack of facial stripes.

YOSEMITE VALLEY

Glaciers account for some of North America's most magnificent alpine scenery. They form where there is abundant snowfall and summer temperatures low enough to allow the accumulated snow to persist. Glaciers scrape huge amounts of material from the sides and bases of canyons, forming U-shaped valleys, knife-edged ridges, great amphitheaters and hanging canyons decorated with waterfalls.

The most famous of the Sierra Nevada's glacier-carved canyons is Yosemite Valley, where 3,000-foot-high granite cliffs tower above the meandering Merced River. The Valley is a mosaic of riparian, or stream-side habitat, meadows, oak woodlands and the nearby mixed coniferous forests of ponderosa pine, incense cedar and Douglas fir.

In the Sierra Nevada, yellow-breasted chats keep to the thickets that grow along foothill streams which can reach as far as Yosemite Valley in the late summer. They forage in the low vegetation for insect swarms, occasionally eating fruits and seeds. Yellow warblers breed in the Valley, building nests between the forking stems of low shrubs.

Other perching birds, or passerines, found in Yosemite Valley's mixed coniferous forests include the solitary vireo, and black-throated gray and yellow-rumped warblers. Because they adapt their diet, eating mostly insects in the summer but feeding off seeds and berries in the colder months, yellow-rumped warblers are the only warblers that commonly reside in the Sierras all the year round.

Below: Half Dome by the Merced River. Granite domes are common in the Yosemite region of the Sierra Nevada. Niagara River, connecting Lake Erie to Lake Ontario, plunges over Niagara Falls (facing page) to enter seven-mile-long Niagara Gorge.

EASTERN CANYONS

Except in the southern states, ice sheets gave eastern canyons much of their character, reshaping, redirecting and even reversing the drainage patterns of some rivers. Until a glacier blocked its route, Pennsylvania's Pine Creek drained through a broad valley into the Tioga River. Forced to find another route during the last ice age, it formed the Pine Creek Gorge, which cuts through fifty miles of the Appalachian Plateau of north central Pennsylvania and is up to 1,000 feet deep. The Niagara Gorge, which runs for seven miles beyond Niagara Falls, marking the United States-Canada boundary, is another ice-age creation.

Glaciers played no role in the formation of the deepest of all eastern canyons, Linville Gorge. This 2,000-foot-deep chasm was carved by the Linville River as it cascaded down the east slope of the Blue Ridge of western North Carolina.

As the Hudson River carves through the Highlands of the Appalachian Range in New York State, it forms the Hudson Valley. The Highlands are interesting both geologically, as they consist of some of the oldest rock in North America, and biologically as a place of transition, a meeting place for plants and animals from the north and south of the country.

The higher elevations of the Highlands provide habitats for northern birds, such as the Blackburn warbler and the brown creeper. The Carolina wren, the largest wren of eastern North America, is a southern species which has established itself along the Palisades of the lower Hudson Valley. Another southern species, the fish crow, favors coastal marshes and beaches but can be found inland along the Hudson.

THE LAST REFUGES

For the early European settlers, the American mountains stood as barriers to settlement, travel and trade – but also because they are inconvenient for settlers, these wrinkles in the earth's surface have been spared much of the wholesale change suffered by the surrounding lowlands. Relatively unaffected by the spread of civilization, mountains have become refuges, places where animals have been driven to by humans.

At the headwaters of the Yellowstone River, where the Rocky Mountains cut through the northwest corner of Wyoming, lies the greatest concentration of geysers anywhere in the world. Established in 1872, Yellowstone National Park, along with Yosemite, marked the first time that any government set aside land to protect and preserve a wild place. Today, Yellowstone National Park contains one of the richest concentrations of wildlife anywhere in the United States. Over 15,000 elk graze the park's plateaus and meadows, sharing them with one of the world's largest buffalo herds.

Grizzlies, a park attraction second only to the geysers, and Yellowstone National Park are firmly linked in the public's mind. As recently as the early 1970s bears fed at open dumps within the park. Inevitably, as the grizzlies became accustomed to man and his food, conflicts between people and bears increased. When the dumps were closed, scores of "problem" grizzlies disappeared from the greater Yellowstone area.

Like almost all big, North American predators, the grizzly was once far more numerous and widespread than it is today. At one time it roamed over much of the West, ranging from the Pacific to the Great Plains and as far south as Mexico. As the area was settled, the grizzly was systematically eliminated. Still common in Alaska, there are fewer than 1,000 bears remaining in the forty-eight conterminous states. Today, grizzlies are limited to a few northern areas, among them the Yellowstone area of Wyoming and Montana and the Glacier National Park area of Montana. The grizzly is one

of two varieties of brown bear native to North America; the other is the Kodiak bear, which is limited to three islands off the Alaskan coast.

Grizzlies are found in open country in meadows and woodlands. However, in the forest they are superseded by the smaller black bear. The home range of a grizzly bear is among the largest of any land mammal. Adult males range, in exceptional cases, over territories covering up to 1,100 square miles. Grizzlies hibernate in dens during winter for approximately five months. In Montana and Wyoming, den sites are situated at altitudes above 6,500 feet and usually face north so that sufficient snow remains throughout the winter to blanket the den entrance.

Facing page: (top) the Yellowstone River crashing through isolated back country in Yellowstone National Park, and (bottom) elk crossing the Snake River in Grand Teton National Park. Bull elk control large harems during the fall rut. Top right: grizzlies exploiting the annual salmon run in Brooks River, Alaska. Right: Old Faithful Geyser, Yellowstone National Park.

WILDERNESS AND WILDNESS

Creating wilderness parks has proved far easier than preserving their wildness. Well into its second century, Yellowstone National Park has become a wilderness island increasingly constricted by civilization. Though the park is vast, it does not include the entire Yellowstone ecosystem. Attempts to reintroduce the gray wolf, once perceived as a threat to big game populations, are opposed by cattle and sheep ranchers who border the park.

Some of North America's most grand and scenic canyons now lie under water. Hetch Hetchy Reservoir, serving the water needs of thousands of San Franciscans, overlies a canyon as spectacular as Yosemite.

As they migrate north, sandhill cranes gather in spectacular numbers every March along a seventy-mile stretch of the Platte River in Nebraska. The city of Denver has plans for dams that would forever alter these wetlands.

There were once serious plans, now long abandoned, to use the Grand Canyon as a reservoir. While the Canyon remains wild, Lake Powell, the dam of which is just upstream of the canyon, has changed the Colorado forever. The dam has eliminated seasonal floods and allowed a thriving, riparian woodland community to establish itself alongside the River. Birds such as the willow flycatcher, hooded oriole and blue grosbeak, which now nest in the canyon, were unknown in the area before the construction of the dam.

Nearly extinct by 1900, the American bison (below) managed to survive only in the mountains of Yellowstone. Facing page top: a young gray wolf. Nearly eliminated in the lower forty-eight states, this wolf is now the subject of a fierce debate over its reintroduction. The Kodiak brown bear (facing page bottom) is a type of grizzly that lives on Alaska's Kodiak Island. Overleaf: the ancient forest peaks of Olympic National Park.